KANSAS PACIFIC

An Illustrated History

by Robert Collins

Contents

Title Page: This famous Kansas Pacific photograph by Robert Beneke shows employees posing with seven diamond-stacked 4-4-0's and one 0-4-0 at the KP's roundhouse in Armstrong (Kansas City), Kansas, circa 1874. The well-polished machines, from left to right, are Nos. 85, 86, 60 (an 0-4-0), 21, 6, 88, 17 and 32. Engine 21 formerly bore the name "Seminole," while No. 17 was formerly the "Choctaw." Photo from the Beneke collection, DeGolyer Library, Southern Methodist University, in Dallas, Tex.

Page Three: This Union Pacific, Eastern Division advertisement was selling the road's service to Denver and the West even before the tracks had made it past Junction City, Kansas. Collection of the Nebraska State Historical Society.

Copyright 1998 by South Platte Press.
All Rights Reserved.

First edition October 1998.

ISBN 0-942035-46-1

Published by
South Platte Press
Box 163, David City, NE 68632

Printed by
Service Press
Box 606, Henderson, Ne 68371

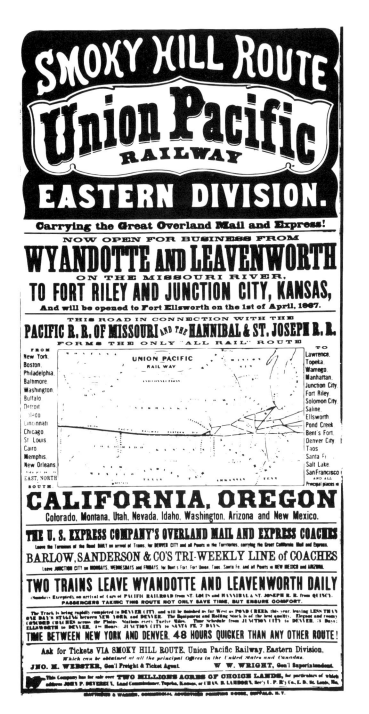

Foreword

This book tells the story of Kansas' first great railroad, the Kansas Pacific. And I do mean that; it isn't just hype. The story of the KP involves dramatic characters, furious battles, and savage terrain. This book will present that story with the passion it deserves.

The KP's main line ran from Kansas City to Denver, connecting two of the most important cities of the central U.S. It opened the era of the "Wild West," then brought some of the first settlers to western Kansas. The KP's story sometimes gets lost next to its large competitor, the Union Pacific. This book will try to set the record straight.

I like to know your reaction to my books, and this one is no exception. You may send your comments to me at Post Office Box 134, Andover, Kansas 67002. I can't guarantee a reply, but you never know.

I had help with this book, and I'd like to give thanks to those who have made it possible. First and foremost, thanks must go to Mike Boss; he encouraged me to undertake this project, he provided scads of research material, and if he hadn't asked, I wouldn't have written it. I'd also like to thank everyone at the Kansas State Historical Society for helping to locate material and photographs. And I'd like to thank the Denver Public Library, the DeGolyer Library, and the Union Pacific Museum for allowing the use of photographs from their collections.

And, as always, I'd like to thank you, the reader, for your support and interest. Without you, we writers would be a pretty sorry lot.

Robert Collins
Andover, Kansas

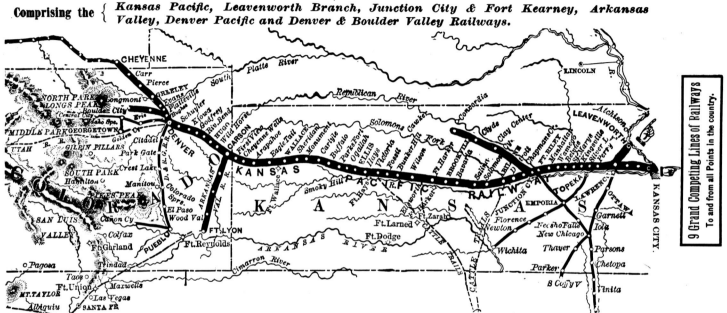

MAP OF THE KANSAS PACIFIC RAILWAY,
AND OPERATED LINES.

Comprising the { Kansas Pacific, Leavenworth Branch, Junction City & Fort Kearney, Arkansas Valley, Denver Pacific and Denver & Boulder Valley Railways.

9 Grand Competing Lines of Railways
To and from all Points in the country.

KANSAS PACIFIC RAILWAY } From Kansas City and Leavenworth, through Kansas and Colorado to Denver and the famous resorts of the Rocky Mountains.

Splendid Mountain Scenery, Pike's Peak, Gray's Peak, Perpetual Snow, Good Hotels, Pure Air, Crystal Streams, Beautiful Cascades, Hot and Cold Soda Springs, Sulphur and Chalybeate Springs; Gold, Silver, Copper, Lead, Iron and Coal Mines; Pleasant days with Cool nights.

This detailed map of the Kansas Pacific shows the rail system at its peak, circa 1872. Early KP timetables listed the distance between Kansas City and Denver at 639 miles. Kansas State Historical Society.

The Vision

When the United States was founded in the 1780's, most of its citizens lived along or close to the Atlantic Coast. A few hardy souls had crossed the Appalachian Mountains to establish villages. Over the next four decades their numbers grew. Towns sprouted up along the Ohio, Tennessee and Mississippi rivers. In 1821, when Missouri was admitted as a state, the western edge of the country reached the confluence of the Kansas and Missouri rivers.

Railroads were still a curiosity limited to Britain at this time. Few men of influence even considered bringing this transportation marvel to the New World. Some, including an Ohio school board, believed that railroads were the tool of Satan and that man was not meant to travel at the unholy speed of 15 miles an hour. And yet, as early as 1820, architect and engineer Robert Mills published a treatise suggesting that a railroad could be built to the Pacific Ocean. Nothing came of this proposal and the notion was set aside.

The 1840's saw public attitudes in America begin to change. The first "boom" in railroad building was underway. Many now realized that railroads could free commerce from relying on slow-moving rivers to transport goods. The more visionary saw in railroading the potential to open up the vast interior of the country to white settlement. Most importantly to the story of the Kansas Pacific, two men again suggested building a railroad to the Pacific Ocean.

This time one of the two, Dr. Hartwell Carter, went to Washington, D.C., to lobby Congress on the idea. He met Asa Whitney, a New York businessman whose trade took him to China. In 1845 Whitney took up Carter's idea and proposed a land-grant railroad built by emmigrants. Whitney's idea was dismissed at first, but when Texas and the Southwest became American territory, it became a national issue.

But now the issue of slavery began to divide the nation. Compromise after compromise failed to cool tensions. Books like *Uncle Tom's Cabin* inflamed those both in favor of and against slavery. When Kansas Territory was opened to settlement in 1854, partisans from both sides dashed in. Blood was shed time and again as the question of whether Kansas would become a free or slave state was determined.

One of the few issues agreed upon by the factions was the matter of railroads. Although the Kansas Territorial Legislature was described by abolitionists as the "Bogus Legislature," when the body passed bills to incorporate railroad companies, it was hailed as progressive. Many of these companies were "paper railroads," doomed never to be built due to lack of financial support. But several did gain backing and were actually constructed.

One of the first companies incorporated was the Leavenworth, Pawnee & Western in 1855. The tracks of this road were to extend from Leavenworth, one of the state's first cities, to the Fort Riley area of north-central Kansas. The books were opened to stock sales late in 1856, whereupon a group of prominent Kansans associated themselves with the project. However, their efforts failed to obtain investors. A second group tried again, this time with the immediate goal of building from Leavenworth to the new abolitionist city of Lawrence. They negotiated for land from the Delaware and Pottawatomie Indians. Still, there were no takers.

KANSAS TRAILS . . . .

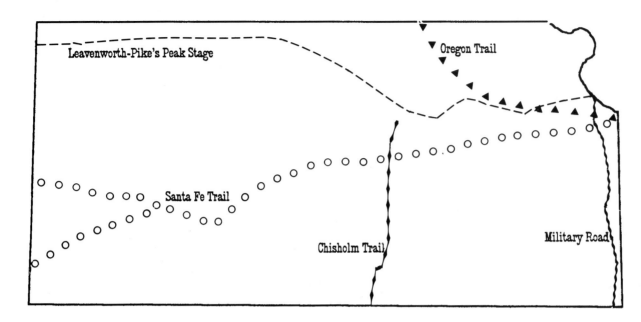

Leavenworth-Pike's Peak Stage

Oregon Trail

Santa Fe Trail

Chisholm Trail

Military Road

FORTS IN KANSAS . . . .

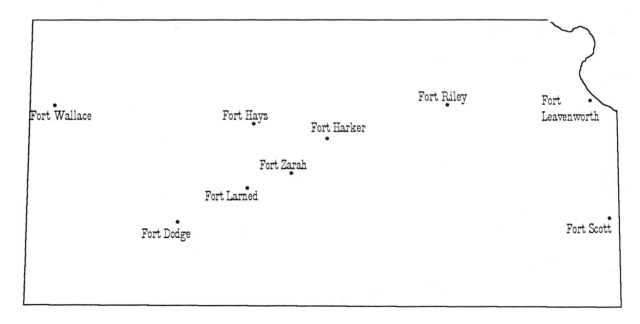

Fort Wallace

Fort Hays

Fort Riley

Fort Leavenworth

Fort Harker

Fort Zarah

Fort Larned

Fort Dodge

Fort Scott

In the meantime, the idea of a railroad to the Pacific became caught up in the slavery issue. Northerners opposed to slavery wanted an eastern terminus of the road in the North. Slave states of the South demanded a southern city have that honor. Nothing was settled until the Civil War broke out in 1861. With the South out of contention, the matter of an eastern terminus was decided quickly. The Pacific Railway Act of 1862 called for the line to begin at Omaha, Nebraska, with a plan to eventually connect Chicago with the western terminus at San Francisco. Building east from California would be the Central Pacific, a road then already organized. Building west would be a new company: the Union Pacific.

Backers of the LP&W saw potential for their line in the Railway Act. Allying themselves with interests in St. Louis, they obtained a land grant as part of the act.

They presented plans calling for two routes out of Leavenworth. Both would roughly follow the Kansas River west, with one heading west along the Solomon River and the second northwest along the Republican River. Government support favored the Republican route, and that became an official part of the LP&W project. The road was obliged to construct 100 miles of track within two years.

The company hired a contract firm and work began in late 1862, but financial troubles soon stalled construction. In an effort to secure backing, the LP&W's backers met with officials of the newly-created Union Pacific in hopes of allying the two roads.

Then John C. Fremont and Samuel Hallett entered the picture.

ABOVE OPPOSITE: This map illustrates the major trails that were in use in Kansas before and during construction of the UPED-KP. The Military Road connected military outposts at Forts Leavenworth, Scott and Gibson (in Oklahoma). The Santa Fe Trail was a commercial trail generally used by freighters, while the Oregon Trail was used mainly by pioneer settlers. The Chisholm Trail was created after the Civil War and used for the cattle drives from Texas. The Leavenworth-Pike's Peak Stage trail was one of several similar routes to gold mines around the Denver area during the gold rush of 1859. Author's illustration.

BELOW OPPOSITE: This map shows the U.S. Army forts that existed in Kansas during the time that the UPED-KP was built. The railroad would eventually tie together five of the outposts: Leavenworth, Riley, Harker, Hays and Wallace. This linkage proved immensely beneficial for both the Kansas Pacific and early town settlers during their struggle with the Indian tribes of Kansas. Author's illustration.

LEFT: Samuel Hallett was the driving force behind the early efforts of the UPED. Some historians have contended that, had he not met a premature death, the UPED may very well have beat the Union Pacific to the 100th meridian and gone on to become the eastern half of the first transcontinental railroad. **Kansas State Historical Society.**

BELOW: A builder's photo of the UPED locomotive "Seminole" hints at the decoration, elaborate lettering and bright colors that were applied to some steam engines of the era. Built by the Rogers Locomotive Company in 1867, this 4-4-0 was later assigned the number 21. Note the tender lettering, indicative of the practice then to use "r.w." to abbreviate "railway." **Nebraska State Historical Society.**

A Contentious Man

John C. Fremont was famous as an explorer of the American West. He was the first presidential nominee of the anti-slavery Republican Party. And his father-in-law was Missouri Senator Thomas Hart Benton, who had long supported western railroads. As early as the 1820's, Benton had sponsored legislation to survey a transcontinental line. He became a vital backer of the Pacific Railroad of Missouri (later the Missouri Pacific) during the 1850's.

Samuel Hallett was a man with a proven record of railroad-related accomplishments. As a New York investment banker, he helped insure the success of the Atlantic & Great Western line between Salamanca, New York, and Dayton, Ohio (later part of the Erie Railroad). He had connections with railroad financiers in both America and Europe. And Hallett was still only in his mid-thirties. Here was a man of vigor and vision.

Fremont and Hallett acquired control of Leavenworth, Pawnee & Western stock in May 1863. Fremont was elected president while Hallett became general superintendent and sole construction contractor. At this time the LP&W was renamed the Union Pacific Railway Company, Eastern Division. Although not owned by Union Pacific, this name was apparently chosen to imply that the road was a contender for the transcontinental route. Indeed, initial plans called for the UPED to build to Ft. Kearny, Nebraska, then west along the proposed Pacific Route. Hallett cast off the former contractors and began to actively promote his new company, confident that it could win the transcontinental race.

Hallett's first fight came soon after coming aboard. Leavenworth was still the planned starting point for the line. The city was the largest in Kansas at the time. Its mainstays were nearby Fort Leavenworth, vital to the Union war effort, and the Missouri River trade. However, the community's promoters believed that any railroad had to come to them – not vice versa.

Hallett went to Leavenworth city officials in August and asked them to purchase some $100,000 in UPED stock. The leaders dithered and dickered. Hallett then decided that, if they wouldn't play by his rules, he'd move the starting point to another community.

He chose the village of Wyandotte (now Kansas City, Kansas). Although not much of a town, Wyandotte was ideally placed. The Kansas River flowed into the Missouri here, meaning that the new road would be close to its supply point and able to build directly west along the Kansas. Across the state line were the up-and-coming railroad terminals of Kansas City and Independence. Best of all, in Hallett's view, the leaders of Wyandotte were willing to meet his terms.

Hallett secured enough material to build 50 miles of track and offered $1.50 a day for laborers. A ground-breaking ceremony was held in Wyandotte on September 7, 1863. By November, 40 miles of grading were completed and hopes were high that trains would soon be running to Lawrence.

However, a river packet carrying rail became ice bound and this material was not delivered until February. The first UPED locomotive had previously arrived in the area in December. Also on board was the road's first conductor, Moses Brinkerhoff, who was moderately famous for having foiled a train robbery on the Panama railroad in 1855.

LEFT: John C. Fremont provided the political backing to get the UPED started. He would also be the catalyst for the road's first internal strife. **Kansas State Historical Society.**

BELOW: Locomotive No. 17 (formerly the Choctaw) was photographed switching cars at Wyandotte, Kansas, during the early years of the UPED. Ground had first been broken here for the road on September 7, 1863. Wyandotte was merged with two other towns in 1886 to form Kansas City, Kansas. **Kansas State Historical Society.**

Progress was impressive, considering that the Civil War had created a labor shortage in the area and some workers had to be brought in from Canada. The first rails were finally laid in April 1864. The UPED thereafter recorded the first railway accident in Kansas when the locomotive "Wyandotte" was partially dunked into the Missouri River. Little damage resulted and work continued.

Then Hallett got into a feud with his boss, John Fremont, who had apparently come under the sway of the other Union Pacific. The two roads were now competitors, each hoping to reach the Central Pacific before the other. (A July 1864 amendment by Congress to the Pacific Railway Act implied that the first railroad to reach the 100th meridian would receive the right of way to meet the CP.) Clearly, the Kansas road could not have its rival in any position of control. Hallett maneuvered to get Fremont removed from the company's board of directors. Subsequently, Hallett, along with St. Louis banker John D. Perry, were in sole control of the UPED.

The first UPED excursion was held in late April 1864. By July it appeared the first 40 miles would be completed and the line from Wyandotte to Lawrence opened to freight and passenger traffic. Hallett prepared for a gala celebration on August 18. Then word got out that the UPED might lose its government subsidy due to a claim of shoddy track work.

The allegation had been made to President Abraham Lincoln by former UPED engineer O. A. Talcott. He fur-ther claimed that Hallett's company was dishonest and in debt to many. While some of Talcott's accusations may have been true, it was also true that he was a Fremont man, having lost his post when Fremont was ousted. It seems certain that Talcott had a grudge against Hallett and the UPED.

Hallett was enraged by Talcott's claims. He told his brother, Thomas Hallett, to insult Talcott the next time he came into the road's Wyandotte office. Thomas Hallett did just this in the summer of 1864; slapping the man and throwing him out into the street. A humiliated Talcott waited until July 27 to get his revenge; by murdering Samuel Hallett.

It was early afternoon when Hallett left a Wyandotte hotel to wire a message. He stopped to talk with a group of people in front of a drug store. As he left the group, Talcott raised a rifle and shot Hallett in the back. He died on the street.

Talcott hastily rode on horseback to his home in Quindaro (now north-central Kansas City, Kansas). Because he had friends in Quindaro and Hallett had enemies, Talcott was never apprehended for the crime.

John Perry, president of the railroad since April, took control of the UPED by forcing Hallett's widow and his brothers to sell off their stock. Many in northeastern Kansas did not believe Perry had what it would take to get the line completed. They feared that Hallett's demise would be quickly followed by that of his railroad.

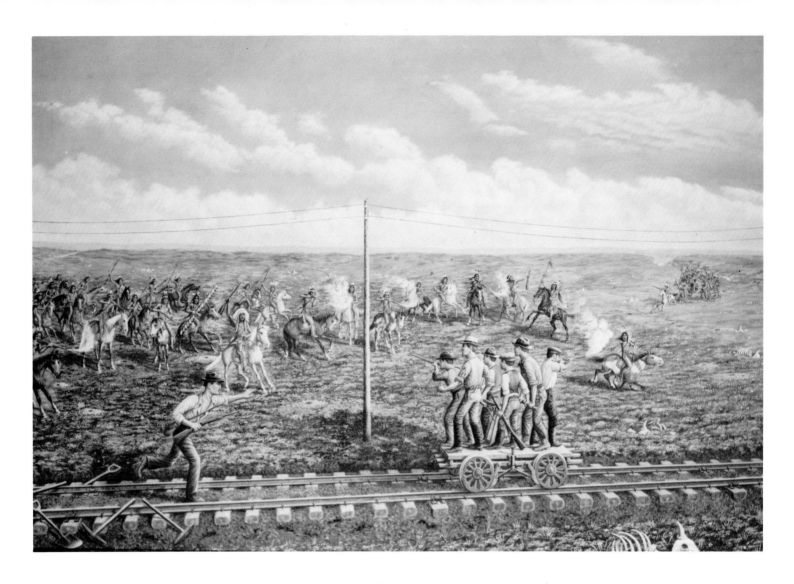

Adolph Roenigk was a German immigrant to Kansas who hired on with the UPED as a track worker. On May 28, 1869, his section crew was attacked by Cheyenne warriors led by Tall Bull at Fossil Creek Station (now Russell). Years later, in 1931, he wrote an article about the incident for the Union Pacific employee magazine. He also commissioned Denver artist J. Gogolin to paint three scenes related to the raid, including this view in which Roenigk makes a dash for an escaping handcar of fellow workers. The Cheyenne, following this attack, would go on to raid settlements in modern-day Lincoln County. **Kansas State Historical Society.**

Troubles and Triumphs

Samuel Hallett's death was a serious setback for the Union Pacific Eastern Division, as were the financial machinations of John Perry. Work was further slowed during 1864 when Kansas came under the threat of invasion by Confederate soldiers and guerillas commanded by General Sterling Price. For a brief period Thomas Durant, head of the Union Pacific out of Omaha, gained some control over one of the UPED's superintendents. However, that man was ousted in early November.

On November 26, 1864, to great acclaim from local citizens, UPED track was laid to the Lawrence depot. The first freight train, carrying barrels of coal oil, arrived December 1; and the first passenger train entered town December 13. An excursion and celebration, postponed from August 18 by Hallett's death, was held in Lawrence on December 19.

The road's next two goals were acceptance by the government of the first 40 miles and laying rail to Topeka. The former was achieved when President Andrew Johnson accepted the "first forty" on October 30, 1865. Topeka was reached December 29, 1865, whereupon another grand celebration took place. Track crews kept working by heading for Junction City.

Meanwhile, a survey party was sent west out of Fort Riley. Their charge was to plot the best route to a new destination for the railroad: Denver. By then it was obvious that the UP out of Omaha would win the race for the 100th meridian. UPED President John Perry decided it was advantageous to target a more financially promising destination than Fort Kearny in Nebraska. The standing acts of Congress stipulated that the road should follow the Republican River. A few, however, felt that the Smoky Hill Valley would be a far more direct route to Denver, and construction through the valley would be easier.

Construction proceeded apace. Even as crews of the contractor Shoemaker, Miller & Company were building west, a branch from Lawrence to the south side of Leavenworth was completed in the spring of 1866. Wamego became an end-of-track town in June 1866. Manhattan was achieved at the end of August and Junction City was finally reached in early November. From there, the UPED would be entering a virgin frontier mostly devoid of settlements.

That summer the route was officially changed to follow the Smoky Hill River. The survey party had returned with a plan that would have the road first head for the isolated village of Salina. The track would pass the small U.S. Army post of Fort Harker, followed by Fort Hays. It would then enter the country of three nomadic Indian tribes: the Cheyenne, Arapahoe and Kiowa. In a report to Kansas Governor Samuel Crawford on January 17, 1867, UPED Superintendent W. W. Wright stated that the line was 20 miles west of Fort Riley and that construction to the 285th milepost (near present-day Hays) would be completed by the end of 1867.

During the first half of 1867 track work proceeded at lightning speed, the flat terrain presenting few construction obstacles. Abilene was reached in late March despite blizzards and flooding. The rails hit Salina around April 20. Crews were laying track at the rate of a mile and a half per day.

Then the Indian raids began. The Cheyenne, Arapahoe, Kiowa and Commanche tribes had been attacking

ABOVE: This view purports to show UPED surveyors at rest in their camp in western Kansas during 1867. The firearms visible were then deemed as vital to their job as surveying equipment. Protection was otherwise being provided by a contingent of black soldiers from the 38th U.S. Infantry, posed at left, while teamsters and cooks are at right. Kansas State Historical Society.

LEFT: The vulnerability of UPED track workers to Indian attacks and other dangers is apparent in this view of a section crew aboard their hand car near Salina. Photographer Gardner noted that the unimpeded view to the flat and distant horizon was five miles. Although the railroad provided its employees with carbines and cartridges, this hardened bunch was apparently not anticipating any trouble. Kansas State Historical Society.

This view of a UPED construction train, believed to have been taken west of Fort Hays, illustrates the equipment typical of the period. The train was both home for the workers and a refuge from possible Indian attrack. It was otherwise a magnet for the unruly denizens of the "Hell on Wheels" towns that sprang up as construction moved west. Gardner collection, Kansas State Historical Society.

This is one of two nearly-identical and often-published Gardner photographs that show the UPED tracklaying crew in action east of Ogallah. Note some of the ties at left are essentially pointed logs. The large tub car directly behind the locomotive provided extra water for the engine until on-line water tanks were constructed. Gardner collection, Kansas State Historical Society.

Alexander Gardner, noted for his photography work during the Civil War, traveled the length of the UPED in the fall of 1867 taking sterioscopic views of track construction, towns and landscapes. Here Gardner captured a bucolic scene of the poorly-built UPED tracks curving along the banks of the Kansas River near Fort Riley. Track conditions often limited passenger train speeds to less than 20 miles per hour. Union Pacific Museum.

ABOVE: Many of the early UPED station buildings were similar to the austere Junction City depot, one of the "big shacks" that the road was derisively known for. Following the railroad's arrival in late 1866, Junction City was generally acknowledged as the dividing point between "civilization" to the East and "untamed frontier" to the West. Gardner collection, Kansas State Historical Society.

LEFT: The UPED's wooden truss bridge is pictured spanning the Republican River near Junction City. The susceptibility of such structures to damage from flash floods during the early years of construction greatly slowed progress and drained the road's financial resources. Gardner collection, Kansas State Historical Society.

CHEYENNE INDIANS ATTACKING A WORKING PARTY ON THE UNION PACIFIC RAILROAD, August 4, 1867.—[Sketched by T. R. Davis.]

ABOVE: Kansas Governor Samuel Crawford was an early supporter of the UPED. He also persuaded the U.S. Army to provide protection for work crews during the violent summer of 1867. Kansas State Historical Society.

TOP OPPOSITE: A lithograph from Harper's Weekly for September 7, 1867, illustrated a Cheynne Indian attack upon a UPED track grading crew. Accounts of Indian incursions against the railroad included an unsucccessful siege by Kaw warriors of the Brookville locomotive roundhouse after the town's residents had taken refuge there. Kansas State Historical Society.

BOTTOM OPPOSITE: Troops were photographed while on review at Fort Harker in 1867. It was from here that the Army's 1867 campaign was instigated against the Indian tribes attacking the Kansas Pacific. The railroad town of Ellsworth was established four miles from the fort. Union Pacific Museum collection.

RIGHT: A sample of 1869 correspondence from a U.S. Army officer at Fort Wallace to his commanding officer concerns one of the many fatal skirmishes between Native Americans and Kansas Pacific workers. Note the reference to George Custer, who actively served in the region during the Army's campaign to force the Southern Plains tribes onto reservations. Fort Hays Historical Museum.

May 30, 1869

To: Bvt. Brig. Gen. Chauncey McKeever
    Asst. Adjt. Gen. Dept. of the Mo., Ft. Leavenworth

General,

I have the honor to inform you that a party of from thirty to sixty Indians crossed the R.R. track, on the 25th instant at Fossil Creek, twenty eight miles east of this point. they wounded four men at that Station and killed two at the water tank, which is about three miles west from that station.

The Indians cut down part of the telegraph wire, cut it into small pieces and filled the bodies of the dead men with them. They arranged the switch so as to throw the cars off the track, causing much damage to the train. The train due at 2:20 a.m. yesterday arrived at Hays between 5 and 6 a.m. to-day. The first intimation I had of the affair was this morning. The detachment sent out by General Custer will probably obtain more definite information than I can give at present.

I am General
Very Respectfully
Your Obt. Svt.
Samuel Overshine, Capt. 5th Inf., Commanding

TOP OPPOSITE: Salina, later to be the largest city in north-central Kansas, looked very roughhewn in this Gardner photograph. The depot sits at left while the large building under construction was a hotel operated by former Civil War nurse Mary "Mother" Bickerdyke. In Kansas she became known for her social aid to Civil War veterans who came here to farm. Gardner collection, Kansas State Historical Society.

BOTTOM OPPOSITE: Hays City was little more than a collection of tents in this 1867 view. This location was favored by the railroad's townsite company over the competing town of Rome, of which "Buffalo Bill" Cody was a co-founder. A good water supply source helped to assure the future of Hays City. Gardner collection, Kansas State Historical Society.

ABOVE: The strategic benefit of the UPED to Army outposts in Kansas is seen in this 1867 view of the siding at Fort Harker, jammed with carloads of supplies for the garrison. The ample land grants that railroads like the UPED received from the U.S. government were repaid in the form of discounted freight rates for the military. Gardner collection, Kansas State Historical Society.

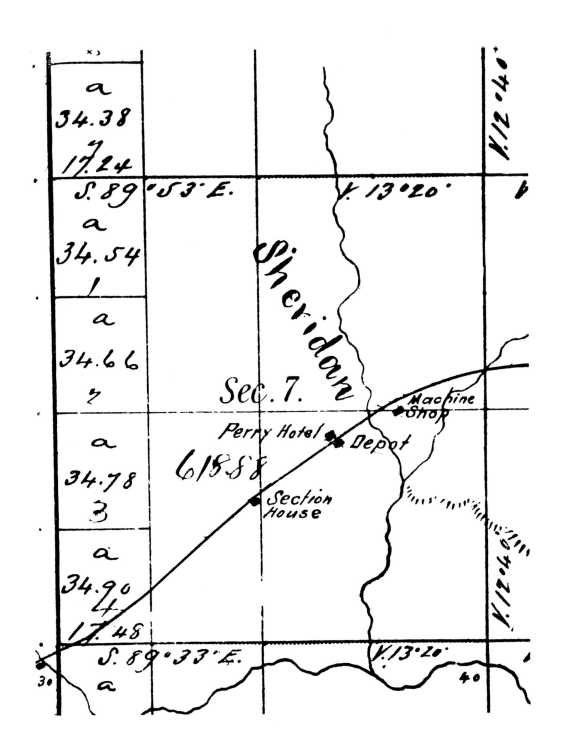

a
34.38
7
17.24

S. 89°53' E.   V. 13°20'   b

a
34.54
1

a
34.66
7

Sec. 7.

Sheridan

Machine Shop

Perry Hotel   Depot

a
34.78
3

61588

Section House

a
34.90
4
17.48

30   a

S. 89°33' E.   V. 13°20'   40

V. 12°40'

V. 12°45'

There are apparently no known photographs of Sheridan from its days as the end-of-track Soddom and Gamorrah of the UPED. (It was named for famed Union Army officer General Phil Sheridan.) This survey map from the Kansas State Auditor's office gives some idea regarding the location of railroad facilities at Sheridan, located 405 miles west of Kansas City. Today there are no visible remains of the town. Kansas State Historical Society.

whites in western Kansas since the Sand Creek Massacre in Colorado in 1864. A peace conference near the Little Arkansas River in 1865 failed to stop the violence. As the UPED survey and construction crews moved west, they became part of the bloody struggle. The U.S. Army in Kansas, under the command of General William T. Sherman, did nothing. On June 21 Robert Shoemaker, head of the construction crews, sent word to Governor Crawford that four men had been killed in an attack. On June 24 UPED President John Perry reported that three men were killed and scalped within 20 miles of Fort Harker, while Shoemaker reported two more killed near Bunker Hill.

Governor Crawford responded to these reports vigorously. He asked Secretary of War Edwin Stanton and General Sherman to deploy more soldiers and to call up a volunteer force. Sherman was hesitant, so on July 1 Crawford issued a proclamation to raise eight companies of cavalry. These companies became the 18th Kansas Cavalry Regiment. Once organized, the regiment rode to Fort Harker to join the 10th U.S. Cavalry and a battalion of the 7th Cavalry. These forces skirmished with the Indians throughout the summer.

Finally, on August 21, elements of the 10th Cavalry and the 18th Kansas Volunteers clashed with Native American warriors in the vicinity of northwestern Kansas. The Army's force of about 150 suffered only three casualties, while the Indians may have lost up to 150. This engagement marked the end of the Army's 1867 campaign. However, soldiers of the 38th Infantry continued to guard UPED surveyors and construction workers for the remainder of the year.

The first passenger train arrived at Fort Harker on July 1, 1867. Four months later, in early October, track crews reached the Fort Hays area. Here they found two towns vying to serve both the crews and the fort. The first to be established was Rome, located closest to the fort and co-founded by famed Army scout William F. Cody. By July, Rome had a population of 2,000. The second community, Hays City, was founded a mile to the east by a railroad subsidiary. Hays City won this competition by circumstance. A cholera epidemic devasted Rome in August and the town was vacated soon after the rails arrived.

The spring of 1868 saw the UPED with some 375 miles of track in service. Yet again, Indian raids proved a threat to survey parties and construction crews. This time, however, the Army took the situation seriously. Companies were stationed along the line, mainly from the 38th Infantry. Cavalry patrols were sent to engage warriors before they attacked. By the end of September the trouble had passed and UPED workers in Kansas could carry out their duties without fear.

But on September 5, 1868, work stopped; not on account of the wrath of Native Americans, but from lack of funds. A new contract and additional subsidies from Congress would not come until it went back into session, so the crews were discharged. The railhead ended at Sheridan, a village along the Smoky Hill River some nine miles southwest of present-day Winona.

Sheridan became one of the toughest towns in Kansas. Congregating here were soldiers from nearby Fort Wallace, buffalo hunters and railroad employees waiting to resume work. The town was otherwise a stage stop and became an overland freight shipment point for wagon trains to Colorado, New Mexico and Arizona. Sheridan also attracted gamblers after easy money, prostitutes hoping to give a good time, and outlaws searching for a hiding place. More than 30 men were hanged, usually on a railroad trestle over a dry wash east of town. In all, close to 100 died violent deaths. For almost a year, Sheridan was Hell on Earth.

Kansas Pacific employees strike a pose with 4-4-0 No. 47. Although the location is not known, the lack of trees or hills suggest it was taken somewhere on the High Plains of western Kansas. This classy "American Type" was erected by the Baldwin Locomotive Works in 1870. **Kansas State Historical Society.**

To Denver and Beyond

Even as Sheridan gained a nefarious reputation, work on the Union Pacific Eastern Division had not completely stopped. Survey crews again headed west, laying out the route that the road would take to Denver. Colorado's premiere and growing metropolis had been bypassed by the Union Pacific out of Omaha and the UPED's position appeared to favor it becoming the city's first direct eastern rail connection. Some proposals by UPED executives called for a route that would head west and southwest to Pueblo, then north to Denver. But Denver men lobbied hard for a direct route, and with logic on their side, they won.

In March of 1869 the UPED, by Congressional approval, became the Kansas Pacific Railway Company; the new name reflecting new aspirations. The race for the first transcontinental was by then manifestly won by the Union and Central Pacific lines, culminating in the historic "meeting of the rails" at Promontory, Utah, on May 10, 1869. The Kansas Pacific, however, as some supporters believed, could become the second route to the Pacific Coast.

Construction of the KP resumed that October with William J. Palmer in charge of the work crews. Two shortages faced the new effort: lack of wooden ties and lack of labor. After some wrangling the first problem was settled when the KP hired out Colorado loggers to make pre-cut ties. Getting enough men to lay track took longer to resolve, but eventually there were not only enough workers, but enough to build as expediently as during the construction to Sheridan.

Before the year was out the tracks had entered Colorado. There was a brief return of the Indian raids, with one survey party attacked some 15 miles west of Sheridan. (One of the surveyors, Phillip Howard Schuyler, later received considerable newspaper coverage for his running fight with a large number of pursuing warriors.) This time the raids failed to slow construction progress. On March 30, 1870, the *Rocky Mountain News* reported that the line had reached the old fur trading town of Kit Carson, about 150 miles southeast of Denver.

The KP raced to finish the work by fall. A second crew was hired to build east from Denver, competing with the westbound camp. By August 15, only ten and a quarter miles separated the railheads. The two crews set to work that day, each determined to be the one who would get bragging rights for completing the most track. The east end crew won, driving in the last spike at three o'clock that afternoon on the open prairie east of what is now Strasburg, Colorado. Cheers went up, a special train for executives passed through, and the city celebrated. At long last, Denver was firmly connected to the East.

An antecedent to Denver's joy over the KP's arrival had been the city's first actual rail connection two months earlier. Even as the KP had been preparing to build west, Denver promoters called for a connection northward to the Union Pacific's transcontinental line. During February of 1869, Congress allowed the KP to contract with a new company called the Denver Pacific to build such a line (after the Union Pacific found that it was financially unable to complete the same project). Work proceeded south from Cheyenne, Wyoming, in 1870 and was completed by June 24. The Denver Pacific then became a subsidiary of the KP, as did the Boulder Valley Railroad, a 39-mile line built at about the same time

TOP OPPOSITE: The Denver Pacific was new to Greeley, Colorado, as residents gathered at the simple frame depot for a photograph comparing the two forms of transporation now available to them. Railroad historians have debated whether the 1870 completion of the Denver and Kansas Pacific lines marked the completion of the first "true" transcontinental rail route. By 1869 a railroad bridge had been constructed across the Missouri River at Kansas City, allowing travelers unimpeded connections by rail. Atypically, the first railroad bridge across the Missouri between Omaha and Council Bluffs was not completed until 1872. Rail cars and passengers had to be ferried across the river until then. Union Pacific Museum.

BELOW OPPOSITE: The rail yard at Kit Carson, Colorado, was photographed during the time it was the junction of the Kansas Pacific main line and the KP-controlled Arkansas Valley short line. The AV's 51-mile line to Fort Lyon was envisioned as the start of a KP route to Pueblo and beyond. However, the actions of rail competitors only resulted in its early demise. Beneke collection, DeGolyer Library, SMU.

RIGHT: This sample of a handwritten page from an 1870 era Baldwin Locomotive Works manual explains how Kansas Pacific steam locomotives were to be painted at the factory in Philadelphia. Note how these instructions were carried out on KP locomotive No. 47 (page 24). DeGolyer Library, SMU.

272-C. #120 #121   6/5/69
Pacific R. R. of Kansas

(Tender,) wheels etc. to be dark claret color with plain striping & no scroll work on any part of Engine or tender.
The number to be painted in plain block figures on each side of sand box, on number plate & rear of tender.
The panel on sides of tank to have the initials of the road in plain block letters, separated in the middle by a red panel for the number — #30 — #31

K. P. ◯ R. W.

Engine & tender frames, pump etc. to be painted of a dark green & all loose iron work, brake rods chains etc, to have one coat of Coal tar varnish. Red wheels
Best Brown japan finish.

This well-publicized illustration from the early 1870's depicts a scene at the original Denver Union Station when it served both the Kansas and Denver Pacific lines. Top-hatted gents and parasol-toting ladies observe passenger trains from both roads while the Rockies serve as a backdrop. This facility was replaced by a second Union Station in 1880. Western Collection, Denver Public Library.

from Hughes to Boulder Valley, Colorado.

The Kansas Pacific acquired another subsidiary when it took over the Junction City & Fort Kearney in Kansas. The JC&FK began in 1871, and two years later built from Junction City to Clay Center. Tracks were extended to Clyde in 1878, to Concordia in 1880, and a branch to Belleville was built in 1884.

Next came the Arkansas Valley Railway. It was created with the goal of capturing the freight traffic of southeastern Colorado; and perhaps to also get a jump on the westward aspirations of the Atchison, Topeka & Santa Fe Railway. The AV built a 56-mile line southwest from Kit Carson to Las Animas in the summer of 1873. Plans were made for lines west and northwest to Pueblo, and southwest to Trinidad.

These Colorado lines attempted to forward the ideals proposed for the Kansas Pacific even before work had resumed out of Sheridan. Promoters had tried to enlist Congressional support for turning the former UPED into a transcontinental contender. Proposals were made to extend the line south into New Mexico. From there, tracks could be laid due west to California. However, little enthusiasm was shown in Congress for these schemes and the KP soon forgot about them.

But one man didn't forget. Former KP construction boss William J. Palmer got caught up in the push beyond Denver. When it was clear that the KP had lost interest, Palmer decided to take action on his own. He founded the Denver & Rio Grande Railway in 1870 to connect Denver with El Paso, Texas. The D&RG subsequently became Palmer's narrow-gauge empire, and later a vital standard-gauge Western carrier.

Although now completed, the Kansas Pacific found it still had a lot of work ahead to improve its physical plant. For example, it did not have the most attractive station buildings in the West. The road had initially built rough board-and-batten structures, derisively known as "big shacks," to serve both the freight and passenger trade. The line did later invest in better facilities for some points; such as a three-story brick depot-hotel at Topeka in 1872, and an unusually large and ornate depot for WaKeeney in 1879. The KP also invested in large freight yards at Wyandotte and an extensive shop facility in Denver.

Nonetheless, the carrier's "big shacks" seemed appropriate for the untamed country the KP passed through. This included the rough trade the road participated in during the late 1860's.

This is a very early example of a Kansas Pacific Railway pass, good through the last day of 1870. The recipient of free KP rail travel appears to have been the general superintendent of another railroad. Passes like this were among the perks of being in railroad management. Nebraska State Historical Society.

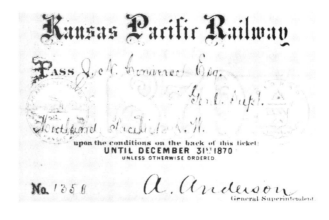

"DANCE - HOUSE."

*Abilene, in its cattle drive days, was a town that rarely slept.
"Dance houses" like the one illustrated here were filled with
rowdy cowboys carrying on with "painted ladies." Kansas
State Historical Society.*

The Real McCoy

Cowboys driving herds of Texas longhorn cattle are the undisputed symbol of the era popularly called the "Wild West." The reality of this era was short-lived; lasting from the late 1860's to the early 1880's. For many, the Atchison, Topeka & Santa Fe Railway is strongly tied to the cattle drives. But it was the Kansas Pacific that first gained the Texas cattle trade, and it was a small town along the KP where the legends of the Wild West first came to life.

Cattle ranching came to Texas early in its history, and by 1860 many ranches covered hundreds of acres and held hundreds of head of longhorn. Texas' seccession and entry into the Confederacy in 1861 affected these ranches in two vital ways. First, the devastation caused by the warring armies of the North and South never came to Texas, allowing herds to grow unchecked. Second, beef markets for Texas cattle were disrupted, while the North's supply of beef cattle were drained. Texans returned from the war facing huge herds of longhorns, perhaps six to ten million head, and a national need for beef.

There was only one problem: no way to get the cattle to consumers. Texas, like most of the South, had sparse rail systems when the Civil War began. The bayou country of the Red River to the east had yet to be penetrated. The western plains were still controlled by hostile Indian tribes. There was no direct route from Texas to the eastern United States.

The only possible hope was to drive the cattle north to Kansas and the closest railroad. But that hope was blocked by quarantine laws. Texas cattle were infested with a tick-like insect that caused "Texas cattle fever," although the longhorns were themselves largely immune to the illness. However, when longhorns were first brought to Kansas during its Territorial period, the "fever" had raged through Kansas cattle herds like a scythe. Thereafter, to protect Kansas herds, the Legislature banned Texas cattle from entering the state.

Illinois businessman Joseph McCoy came to Kansas promoting a solution. He persuaded Governor Crawford that his plan was worthwhile, whereafter the governor persuaded the State Legislature to redraw the quarantine line. McCoy then got word to Texas that cattle could be driven to Kansas along the trail Jesse Chisholm had scouted. McCoy then chose a small town about 25 miles west of Junction City as the end point on the Chisholm Trail where the cattle could then be loaded onto trains.

That small town was Abilene, along the Union Pacific Eastern Division.

The first year of the cattle drives was 1867. McCoy's idea was better than he had anticipated: some 35,000 head of cattle were shipped out of Abilene that year. Within four years, that number had grown to 700,000 head.

But along with the Texas cattle came Texas cowboys. These "cattle punchers" spent long weeks on the trail riding the herd. There was nothing to see except cows and plains. Payday came when they reached Abilene.

After surviving the dangers and monotony of the trail, the cowboys of Abilene wanted to spend their pay and celebrate. They also frequently had time to kill: the cattle were often too thin to ship and needed time to fatten up. Meanwhile, mere moths after the first driving season started, a variety of "undesirables" descended on Abilene,

ABOVE: The man who really tamed Abilene was Marshal Tom Smith. He did it without excessive gunplay or fame. Kansas State Historical Society.

ABOVE RIGHT: The more famous Abilene marshal was "Wild Bill" Hickok. This picture of Hickok was taken at Hays City in 1869. The mild pose is a stark contrast to Hickok's volatile, sometimes violent nature. Kansas State Historical Society.

RIGHT: Photographer Gardner described this 1867 view as showing cattle fording the very-shallow Smoky Hill River at Ellsworth on the Santa Fe Crossing. Nearly identical scenes later took place along the Chisholm Trail as Texas herds were driven to Abilene for shipment via the UPED. The cattle trade would virtually monopolize the railroad's business for about four years, between 1868 and 1872. Kansas State Historical Society.

LEFT: This Gardner photograph from 1867 shows both the railroad siding and "Drover's Cottage" (a hotel for cowboys) at Abilene, as viewed in the distance from the UPED's Mud Creek trestle. The cottage, standing stark against the flat Kansas terrain, preceded the wild cowtown that later sprouted here. Following relocation of the cattle trade to Ellsworth, the Abilene cottage was dismantled and moved there for continued use as a drover's hotel. Gardner collection, Kansas State Historical Society.

RIGHT: The first cattle driven up the Chisholm Trail had arrived only a few weeks before Gardner took this view of cattle cars positioned for loading at McCoy's stock yard in Abilene. Up to 3,000 cattle could be corralled at the Abilene pens. At its peak, the transfer of money in the Abilene cattle trade amounted to about $3 million annually. Such business would not have been available to the UPED under normal conditions of frontier development. Gardner collection, Kansas State Historical Society.

Although this view of 4-4-0 No. 68 and consist was taken during the twilight of the great cattle drive era on the Kansas Pacific, it does illustrate a typical livestock train of that period. The photographer's description indicated this was a train of empty stock cars at Junction City. It was likely westbound for Ellsworth. Beneke collection, DeGolyer Library, SMU.

bringing with them all kinds of diversions. So the cowboys bought liquor, gambled with each other and with professionals, and "danced" with the "soiled doves" in the saloons and brothels. The free flow of booze, the competition for the ladies, and getting conned by gamblers all led to fights. Also, the cowboys were armed with the latest repeating pistols and gunplay often ensued.

At most, about a thousand cowhands were in Abilene at any one time, in a community of a few hundred permanent residents. As late as August 1871, the *Topeka State Record* described Abilene as two communities. North of the KP tracks was "Kansas Abilene," a town of churches, schools and sober citizens. South of the tracks was "Texas Abilene," home to wild cowboys, cheap whiskey, and "...dealers in card board, bone, and ivory."

The righteous citizens of Abilene tried to combat the wickedness of the cattle trade. Incorporation of the city began in late 1869 and led to the first jail being constructed. But local men hired or appointed to bring peace were scared off. Out-of-towners were likewise chased away. The situation appeared grave.

Tom Smith arrived in Abilene in May 1870, interested in the job of town marshal. Although Mayor T. C. Henty wanted Smith, the town trustees did not. But after the Texans destroyed the town jail, the trustees changed their minds. Smith took the job on June 4.

Abilene already had an ordinance against carrying firearms in town. Smith decided that, to get control, the ordinance had to be enforced. Days later a cowboy tried to stand up to the new marshal. Smith snatched the tough's gun and ordered him out of town. Another cowboy tried to intimidate Smith, but he wouldn't yield. Soon cowboys were turning in their guns the moment they entered town. Abilene was at peace.

The cattle drive season ended in October. Later that month, two landowners outside of town got into a dispute and one killed the other. The Dickinson County sheriff and a deputy tried to arrest the murderer, but were scared away. The deputy returned with Smith. The killer and a friend then shot Smith; the man who had tamed Abilene was dead.

Early in 1871 Joe McCoy was elected mayor. He hired James Butler Hickok to be marshal. Hickok already had earned the nickname "Wild Bill," and a reputation to match. He'd previously been marshal of Hays, but had left there when a feud with the brother of his friend, George Armstrong Custer, had escalated to violence. Before that he'd been a bodyguard of the Kansas abolitionist Senator James Lane; a stage driver on the Santa Fe Trail; a scout for the Army; and a buffalo hunter.

Hickok was not the town tamer that Smith had been. He spent most of his time chasing women and gambling. But he was a clever man, and instead of fighting beligerent cowhands, he used his reputation as a sure-shot gunfighter to discourage extreme lawlessness. As the cattle drive season progressed, he and McCoy shut down many of the dance halls and chased away several gamblers. It appeared that Abilene would be able to live with the cattle trade.

But on the night of October 5, a group of Texans started acting wild. Hickok ordered them to behave, but also bought them drinks to prove he didn't have it in for them. Nevertheless, the rowdiness continued. Hickok then confronted the group's leader, a former Confederate soldier who hated the lawman. As the conflict escalated, the two men aimed their pistols at each other and fired. The cowboy grazed Hickok; the marshal killed the Texan.

A nervous Hickok still faced several other cowboys. Just then a man raced into the crowd, startling the marshal. Hickok reacted quickly, but this time the dead man was one of Hickok's own deputies. Within two months Hickok left Abilene for good, discharged by the city. The people of Abilene wondered what would happen in the upcoming year.

The pay car train was once an institution on western railroads like the Kansas Pacific. Such trains were usually operated on a monthly basis in order to distribute wages to those employees living at isolated stations along the line. Here an eastbound pay car train paused at Hays in 1875. Orlando Branham, the Hays depot agent, sits on the locomotive pilot holding his infant daughter. The man standing next to Branham is presumed to be the engineer, Billy Hamilton. Union Pacific Museum.

Quiet Communities

Abilene, while it received the most press then (and now), was not a typical town on the Kansas Pacific. The villages from Junction City westward boomed not because of cattle, but due to the spirit of the sober pioneer.

When the idea of building railroads across the western plains was first bandied about, few thought it possible that anyone could successfully inhabit what was known as the "Great American Desert." The soil was too hard; the climate was too extreme; the "savages" would never be driven off the land. Thousands of settlers crossed the plains before the Civil War, heading for Oregon or California. Few of them seriously entertained the idea of establishing towns on the seemingly-endless prairie.

After the war these ideas began to change. If the railroads could cross the plains, why couldn't towns and farms spring up along the tracks? With railroads in place, goods were easily shipped to and from communities. The accompanying railroad telegraph system expedited communication with the outside world. And with more immigrants coming to America, new towns "out west" were viewed as the solution to overcrowded Eastern cities.

The Kansas Pacific was the first of the western railroads to get caught up in the frontier population boom. It first began selling its land grant property in 1868, with some 111,000 acres sold that year. That figure almost quadrupled the following year.

Much of the KP's territory was still virgin wilderness. This is demonstrated by a directory published circa 1870 in St. Louis. The unknown author had traveled along the completed KP. He described Salina, about 110 miles west of Topeka, as "being on the boundary line of civilization." Ellsworth, an additional 30 miles west, was then just three years old. It had a population of 500, with land sales progressing, but the only public buildings were one church and a schoolhouse. Hays City, the seat of Ellis County, was described as "in the heart of the buffalo and Indian country" and "the only town within a radius of nearly 75 miles."

Most of the KP stations between Salina and the Kansas-Colorado border were listed in the directory as "wood and water" stops. The farthest west towns in Kansas were Sheridan and Pond City. Sheridan, the violent end-of-track town established in 1868, was then accurately predicted as having no chance of permanence. Meanwhile, Pond City (west of present-day Wallace) was described as a small trading post for nearby Fort Wallace. Soliders from this post, consisting mostly of black troopers (otherwise known by their Indian nickname of "Buffalo Soldiers"), were posted at water tanks along the line to guard them against Indian attack.

Within a decade of the directory's publication, full-fledged towns had sprung up along the KP from Abilene to Denver. The open country west of Salina was, by 1880, dotted with farms, ranches, businesses and churches. A major reason for this dramatic change in the landscape was simple: the extermination of the buffalo herds.

Native Americans of the High Plains relied on the buffalo for food, clothing, medicine and virtually every other need. But to the white man, bison meant something else. In number, the ponderous creatures often brought the KP to a halt. One newspaper account from 1867 stated that a buffalo herd three miles long had slowed a passenger train. Bison crossing the right of way at a good pace could easily tear up miles of track.

RIGHT: The man who came to epitomize the lore of the western frontier, William F. Cody, acquired his nickname of "Buffalo Bill" while working for the Kansas Pacific. **Kansas State Historical Society.**

BELOW: A lithograph from Harper's Weekly, dated December 14, 1867, thrilled readers with an artist's rendering of passengers shooting buffalo from aboard a UPED train. The railroad otherwise conducted special buffalo hunt excursion trains for Eastern sportsmen. The most famous of these rail-borne bison hunts involved a visit by the Grand Duke Alexis of Russia. **Kansas State Historical Society collection.**

St. Louis photographer Robert Beneke traveled along the
Kansas Pacific Railway circa early 1874. Like his predecessor,
Gardner, the Prussia-born Beneke recorded both the physical
plant of the Kansas Pacific and the countryside served by the
road. His more memorable images include this scene of a
buffalo hunter's dwelling at Sheridan, which illustrates the
rough living conditions encountered by frontiersmen. Beneke
collection, DeGolyer Library, SMU.

LEFT: This elaborate depot-hotel, built in 1872 from native stone brought in from the Junction City-Manhattan area, was located at Victoria, Kansas. First English, and later Volga-German immigrants, got off here during their attempts to begin new lives in the West. This structure served the railroad until it was razed in 1928. **Kansas State Historical Society.**

BELOW: Robert Beneke provided a more distant view of Victoria in 1874, with the ornate depot-hotel on the eastern horizon. The KP water tower here had originally been tagged as the North Fork water stop. Just out of view at right would have been the gravesites of six UPED track laborers killed in a Cheyenne Indian raid during August 1867. **Beneke collection, DeGolyer Library, SMU.**

ABOVE: Wallace, Kansas, boomed during the 1870's, thanks to abundant rains and the Kansas Pacific. A lesser known fact about Wallace is that famed restauranteur Fred Harvey briefly operated an eating establishment in the Wallace Hotel, the multi-gabled building pictured here. Harvey sold out in 1876 to start a chain of Harvey House restaurants along the Santa Fe system which became synonamous with good food and service. Kansas State Historical Society.

BELOW: With steam locomotives of the period having a limited range of operation before needing to be serviced and fueled, the early Kansas Pacific provided employment opportunity in a number of small towns where locomotive service facilities were established. This Beneke view is treasured by railroad historians for detailing the KP's roundhouse facility at Brookville. Today, no railroad structures remain at this site. Beneke collection, DeGolyer Library, SMU.

RIGHT: Built with local stone, this was the very impressive looking railway hotel at Ellis. Immigrants and emmigrants passing by this large structure undoubtedly thought they were entering a land of milk and honey. However, travelers who stayed here likely found the rooms drafty and the beds hard. Beneke collection, DeGolyer Library, SMU.

LEFT: This heavily-retouched photograph shows one of the more famous oddities of the Kansas Pacific, a sail-powered hand car. Although often identified as being taken at Hays, the background structures suggest the location is actually elsewhere. The man seated at right appears to be Billy Hamilton, the same man as in the Hays pay car photo (page 36). Using the unimpeded winds of the High Plains, an eastbound KP sail car could very well have reached speeds of between 30 and 40 mph--twice that of a passenger train of the time. Accounts suggest that a Wakeeny merchant used a similar sail car to travel to Hays to obtain store supplies. Union Pacific Museum.

The final demise of the buffalo started in the early summer of 1868. Former Army scout William F. Cody challenged another scout, Bill Comstock, to see who could shoot the most buffalo. Cody, riding an experienced hunting pony he purchased from a Ute Indian, killed 69 of the beasts, while Comstock managed only 46. Based on his impressive score, Cody was hired to provide buffalo meat for KP construction crews. It was also here that he apparently gained the nickname "Buffalo Bill." Over the next year and a half, Cody killed more than 4,200 bison.

Decimation of the buffalo came to have both tactical and economical implications. Army officials determined that killing the beasts off would "tame" the Indians by depriving them of their source of survival. A craze for buffalo clothing and leather goods swept the East. Hunters descended on Kansas, mainly working in the southern and western parts of the state. Within just a few years, the shaggy "lords of the plains" were almost completely wiped out. Ironically, the KP used the buffalo as its official symbol on advertisements, maps and stamps.

With the buffalo gone, the KP was free to "civilize" its territory. It promoted town lots and farm spreads to settlers across America and Europe. The road published pamphlets by the tens of thousands, and a quarterly KP newspaper called "The Star of Empire" circulated to some 80,000 readers. It heaped incredible praise on the climate and geography of western Kansas and eastern Colorado. One 1870 handbook even claimed that settlement of the region would favorably moderate the weather. (This was actually a common belief at the time. It was fueled in part by an inadequate knowledge of meterology and by the coincidence of favorable weather during the settlement years of the late 1860's and early 1870's.)

To prove that the land was ideal for settlers, the KP sponsored various agricultural experiment stations. Most of these attempts, funded by either the railroad or private corporations, ended in dismal failure. Much of the climate along the KP was not well-suited to traditional crops and methods. The one great agricultural success, that of a large wheat farm owned by former Abilene mayor T. C. Henry, was then largely ignored by settlers.

However, there were success stories among the new residents founding towns along the KP. The area around Hays thrived with German immigrants from Russia. These German Catholics, who had been invited to Russia by Catherine the Great, had later fled that country in the face of a military draft. After meeting with Kansas Pacific representatives in Europe, many decided to move to Kansas and spent the winter of 1875-1876 in Topeka where they met with KP land agents. These "Volga Germans" went on to establish several towns in Ellis and Rush counties, including those with the reflective names of Liebenthal, Schoenchen, Munjor and Pfeifer. Meanwhile, two Chicago promoters founded the "American colony" (as opposed to an immigrant colony) of Wa-Keeney, which grew spectacularly within a year. Even lonely Wallace, an early division point on the railroad, managed to gain a peak population of 3,500 during the 1880's.

Not all of these efforts resulted in prosperous towns. English businessman George Grant tried to establish a colony in eastern Ellis County in 1873. In his town, Victoria, English settlers tried to recreate their middle and upper-class lifestyles. The English had little luck and Victoria soon became one of the area's Volga German towns. Another effort by Danish immigrants also failed within a matter of weeks, largely because the men in the settlement had no farming experience. Still another movement involved the creation of several African-American settlements in the vicinity of Ellis, the first emmigrants from Kentucky arriving there in September 1877. These black communities were similarly short-lived, with only one, Nicodemus, survivng into the present.

Despite these variegated failures, it could not be denied that the railroad had made the area accessible for settlement. Towns and counties were being created. Farms were dotting the prairie and business appeared lively. Ostensibly, prosperity was on the horizon for the Kansas Pacific.

A view of the Kansas Pacific taxidermy department in Kansas City, Missouri, nicely illustrates the railroad's effort to sell the American frontier to tourists, immigrants and audiences. (Located at the corner of Fifth Street and Broadway, this building also served as the road's headquarters.) The mounted buffalo heads were being prepared for distribution throughout the East, where they served to promote the Kansas Pacific route. Beneke collection, DeGolyer Library, SMU.

Gould's Pawn

Despite its successes, the Kansas Pacific was never on a firm economical footing. The road's financial difficulties began when it lost the lucrative cattle trade to the Atchison, Topeka & Santa Fe Railway. Former Abilene mayor T. C. Henry and a group of local farmers had sent a circular to Texas telling the ranchers they were tired of the cattle trade and its evils. Sure enough, the Texans stayed away from Abilene and a vaccum was created.

Meanwhile, the Santa Fe had reached the Chisholm Trail in 1871. A town was created on Sand Creek in far-northern Sedgwick County. Named "Newton" for the home of several Massachusetts stockholders, the town soon gained the Texas cattle trade. Newton became just as bad a cowtown as Abilene ever was.

But those Newton residents who hated the cattle trade did not have long to complain. Newton's term as a cowboy haven lasted only one season. Officials from the financially-struggling seat of Segwick County, Wichita, lobbied the Santa Fe to build a branch line to their town. Once completed, Wichita's promoters sent word to Texas that they were eager for Lone Star State cattle and cowboys. For the rest of the decade, before the drives ended, the Santa Fe profited from Texas cattle, first at Wichita, then at Dodge City.

The Kansas Pacific did not surrender this trade without a fight. It tried to promote Ellsworth, Brookville, Russell and Ellis as new trail heads. To that end, General Freight Agent T. F. Oakes issued a guide map booklet for the "Ellsworth Cattle Trail." Thousands of copies were apparently distributed, but the effort fizzled. Realistically, no rancher saw a need to drive his cattle across the Santa Fe's tracks, which now stretched from Topeka to the Colorado border.

Another difficulty facing the KP was nature. Reality had caught up with the wild promises. First came the "grasshopper plague" of 1874; acres of crops, trees and other vegetation were eaten by the voracious insects. Farmers became paupers and immigration paused. The region's economy rebounded in the latter 1870's, but then came the drought of 1879-1880. Frustrated homesteaders gave up and moved. Once thriving towns went bust, drying up traffic.

Organized train robbers operating out of Kit Carson, Colorado, also hurt the railroad's financial status. Unlike the more typical hold-up artists, the thieves at Kit Carson stole freight off entire trains. Furthermore, the local justice of the peace, the constable and a KP train guard led the town-wide conspiracy. Activities of the "community gang" were finally stopped during the winter of 1877, but not before thousands of dollars worth of merchandise had been lost.

The Kansas Pacific also had to deal with the poor quality of its track, which did not make for good shipper and passenger relations. It got caught up in a traffic war in Colorado between the Santa Fe and the Denver & Rio Grande. The Arkansas Valley Railway failed to live up to its expectations, being outflanked by the Santa Fe to both Pueblo and Trinidad. (In June 1878, the AV gained the dubious distinction of being the first railroad in Colorado to be fully abandoned.) And while the KP had an ideal routing between two major cities, competition from larger carriers connecting many more cities stunted its growth both in traffic and mileage. The KP's most important western connection was with the Union Pacific

Located approximately halfway between Kansas City and Denver, Ellis was designated a division point on the Kansas Pacific in 1870. Pictured is the original eight-stall roundhouse constructed in 1871, plus the machine shop facility that replaced those located at Ellsworth and Brookville. The town's importance as a division point would extend well into the Union Pacific era. Walter Chrysler, whose father was a KP engineer, was reared in Ellis. Using the mechanical training that he received in the railroad shops, Chrysler later went into the automotive industry and established the Chrysler Corporation. Beneke collection, DeGolyer Library, SMU.

The town of Ellsworth, circa 1874, barely disrupted the far horizon as the stockyards and chutes here awaited the next cattle shipment. After Abilene lost its status as the trail head of the Chisholm Trail, the KP tried to promote Ellsworth as the new staging point. However, this effort was hurt by construction of the Santa Fe Railway through south-central Kansas. Beneke collection, DeGolyer Library, SMU.

"In Case of Emergency. Snow Plow" was how photographer Beneke titled this famous shot of Kansas Pacific 4-4-0 No. 41 equipped with a large wedge plow for bucking drifted snow out of narrow cuts. Often it took two or three – or more – runs at the packed snow for the plow to bust through. On occasion a plow train became stuck or derailed, whereafter shoveling by hand was the last resort. Beneke collection, DeGolyer Library, SMU.

LEFT: Wallace served as an early division point for the Kansas Pacific and boasted the necessary railroad support facilities. Photographer Beneke found KP employees here ready and willing to pose for his wet plate camera. However, one impatient fellow at left moved before the lens was closed, causing a "ghost image." Beneke collection, DeGolyer Library, SMU.

BELOW: Trimmed and shiny 4-4-0's Nos. 79 and 78, the latter westbound, met at the Ellis depot in this Robert Beneke photograph. The mail car directly behind the 78 had apparently been converted into a mobile photography studio which the Kansas Pacific provided Beneke during his tour of the West. This same studio car appears to be attached behind the three locomotives in the snowplow photograph on page 47. Beneke collection, DeGolyer Library, SMU.

INSET: Jay Gould, the famous and often-villified railroad financier, is credited with forcing the Union Pacific's hand concerning the fate of the Kansas Pacific. Union Pacific Museum.

For most of its history, Topeka was a town dominated by the business presence of the Atchison, Topeka & Santa Fe Railway. However, this view shows the impressive Kansas Pacific depot-hotel that served the capitol city. Its appearance belies the poverty then taking down the railroad. Beneke collection, DeGolyer Library, SMU.

Following its 1880 purchase of the KP, the Union Pacific inherited both the promise and the woes of the financially stressed railroad. An example of the latter is this snow blockade that occurred one mile east of Wilson, Kansas, on January 5, 1886. A wedge plow powered by four locomotives was apparently having a hard time opening the narrow cut. This scene could very well have been the Kansas Pacific of just a few years prior. Union Pacific Museum.

at Cheyenne. But by the late 1870's, the UP leadership had little interest in the troubled line.

Jay Gould changed all of that. This railroad financier was energetic, intelligent and – according to his critics – entirely without morals. Born in 1836 at Roxbury, New York, Gould was a leather merchant when he started investing in railroads. He made his fortune by the buying and selling of railroad stock, and by 1874 had become a UP director. However, he soon left the company when one of his stock schemes failed to earn enough of a profit for his tastes.

The episode turned Gould against the Union Pacific. His crusade to crush the road began when he purchased stock of the KP and Denver Pacific, then proposed that the UP consolidate with the two rickety and near-bankrupt lines. Union Pacific saw clearly how disadvantageous Gould's idea would be to its financial health and refused his offer.

Gould then set about to assemble a strong system of regional railroads that could threaten the UP's earnings. He gained control of the Wabash, the Central Branch, the Kansas Central, the Missouri, Kansas & Texas, the Texas & Pacific, the Denver & Rio Grande, and the Denver, South Park & Pacific. The cornerstone to Gould's system was the Missouri Pacific, the KP's principal eastern connection.

Outfoxed by the wily investor, the Union Pacific had no choice but to accept Gould's original offer. Acquiring the KP/DP allowed the Omaha-based railroad to remain competitive by assuming control of new and large service territories in Kansas and Colorado. The consolidation also allowed the UP to have a second connection to eastern roads, other than just at Omaha, by diverting traffic between Cheyenne and Kansas City.

The Union Pacific took control of the Kansas Pacific and its subsidiaries in January 1880, ending about 15 years of independent operation by the one-time transcontinental aspirant. But the merger did not abrogate the KP's problems and the previous fears of UP officials were soon realized. Although purchase of the KP system nearly doubled the size of the UP system, the cost of maintaining the former considerably weakened the UP's financial status. The road otherwise teetered on the edge of insolvency as it expanded its rail line holdings both in Colorado and the Pacific Northwest.

Still, it was the Union Pacific that would have the last laugh on Jay Gould. Always eager for more profits, Gould deferred maintenance on some of his properties to benefit others, (most notably the MK&T in order to enhance the Missouri Pacific). This drove the weaker lines into bankruptcy and their failures took the stronger roads with them. Gould railroads became notorious for their poor physical plant and unsatisfactory service. Meanwhile the Union Pacific, which had reached its lowest point in 1897 by being sold at a receivership auction, acquired new leadership. Edward H. Harriman then quickly turned what had been a mediocre road into the best-maintained rail system in the West.

But by then the Kansas Pacific was largely gone, its territory and physical plant feeling the imprint of its successor. Only the name remained to stir the public imagination when it came to both fact and fiction.

As the reality of the Western frontier gave way to public myths and popular culture concerning the era, the role of the Kansas Pacific in settling the region has occasionally been celebrated. During the 1920's the UP assembled an "oldtime exhibition train" that included No. 943, an aging 4-4-0 "backdated" with a fake diamond stack and cowcatcher pilot. Here the 943 and its vintage-looking passenger consist was at Manhattan, presumably en route to the August 1, 1928, dedication of the restored Kansas territorial capital building located next to the former KP main line at Fort Riley. (Note the old flivver sporting the UP emblem.) Twenty-five years later, in 1953, United Artists released the motion picture "Kansas Pacific" starring Sterling Hayden and Eve Miller. However, the B-grade quality of this Western did little to memorialize the line's early struggles. Union Pacific Museum.

The Legacy

Following its 1880 purchase by the Union Pacific, the Kansas Pacific gradually faded away. Rolling stock was repainted and renumbered. Wooden depots in larger cities like Manhattan and Salina were replaced by brick or stone structures, while the "big shacks" in smaller towns were replaced by UP standard design depots. And, by the arrival of the 20th century, most of the former KP locomotives had been scrapped.

A few artifacts from the KP era remain in Kansas. A mechanic's building in Wamego, consisting of native stone, now houses the Wamego Historical Museum. Similarly, a former KP superintendent's headquarters building in Wallace is being restored by the Fort Wallace Memorial Association. Meanwhile, just south of Victoria are the modestly marked graves of six railroad workers who strayed from the main crew and were killed by raiding Indians in the dark year of 1867. Nothing from the Kansas Pacific remains in Colorado – except perhaps the biggest mystery associated with the railroad.

The saga of KP 4-4-0 No. 51 began on the night of May 21, 1878, when a freight train headed by No. 51 plunged from a bridge over flooded Kiowa Creek some 30 miles east of Denver. Three crew members died, their bodies later recovered downstream. (The nearby town of Kiowa later changed its name to Bennett in honor of the maiden name of two of the widows of those killed.) Salvage workers soon located the remains of the submersed freight cars.

But the locomotive was nowhere to be found. Crews searched for it in the sandy riverbed for at least two months. Early reports claimed that the tender was recovered, but the 4-4-0 had seemingly vanished.

The disappearance of No. 51 has long intrigued railroad enthusiasts and Colorado historians. Enter best-selling thriller author Clive Cussler. Otherwise known for finding wrecked ships, Cussler came to Bennett in January 1989 and led some 200 volunteers in a search for No. 51. The effort failed to find any trace of the evasive engine. Later, after consulting with various railroad historians, Cussler concluded that the 51 had been secretly salvaged in the summer of 1878 after a $20,000 insurance settlement was made, and was thereafter returned to service.

A similar conclusion regarding the engine's retrieval and repair was reached by Loyd Glasier, who wrote of the Kiowa wreck for the 1997 *Colorado Rail Annual*. Glasier noted that a Kansas City newspaper account of late August 1878 supports the salvage claim. The engine was then allegedly rebuilt as a 4-6-0 and continued in UP service for many years.

But questions about the Kiowa Creek wreck remain. Would the KP have spent its precious resources to salvage a wrecked locomotive if an insurance claim had been paid? If the road's owners were trying to scam their insurer, would they have recorded the locomotive's rebuild? And could the KP have salvaged No. 51 in just one night without local residents becoming aware of the activity? The answers remain buried, even if No. 51 did not.

The legacy of the Kansas Pacific, however, is not as elusive. It was the first railroad to build across Kansas and the first to enter Denver from the east. By choosing Wyandotte as its eastern connection, it helped assure that Kansas City, not Leavenworth or Atchison, would

The former Kansas Pacific mechanics building at Wamego, Kansas, stood firm and tree-shaded in the spring of 1997. It is now used by the Wamego Historical Society as part of its museum. Dick Barker, courtesy of Wamego Historical Society.

Showing its age but still holding promise was the former KP superintendent's office and residence at Wallace, pictured in early 1996. The native stone building was used as a section house in its later years of Union Pacific service. It is currently undergoing restoration by the Fort Wallace Memorial Association. Michael Boss.

be the premiere railroad city of the Missouri-Kansas border region.

The KP's opening of the Texas cattle trade at Abilene was the first chapter in the legend of the "Wild West." All the dime novels, movies and television series on the subject owe their basis for creation to Joe McCoy and his railroad of choice.

Also, by having the first rails laid west to Denver, the KP opened a vast area to settlers and their endeavors, triumphant or not. And, undeniably, it played a key role in hastening the decline of Native American culture on the Southern Plains.

For better or worse, the truth and the lies of the era have their origins along the right of way of the Kansas Pacific.

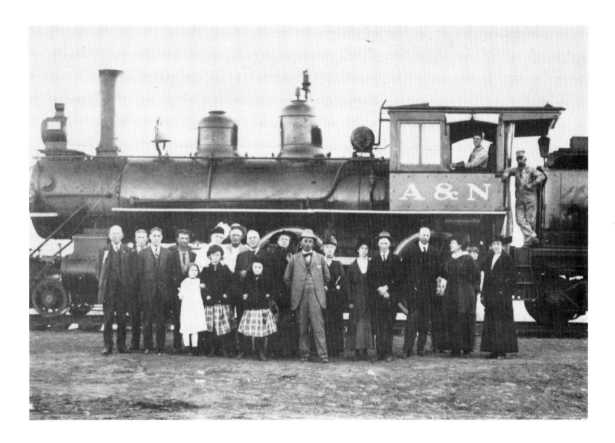

Kansas and Colorado were laced with rail lines in the years following construction of the Kansas Pacific. No doubt many of these projects were aided by seasoned railroaders who had toiled on the early Kansas Pacific. Unlike his better known counterpart, William J. Palmer, another KP veteran who later became his own railroad president was O.P. Byers. Having joined the KP in 1878 as a track worker, Byers eventually inspired to build his own railroad. He accomplished this in the early 1900's when, as president of the Anthony & Northern Railroad, he built a 100-mile short line for hauling Kansas wheat in the vicinity of Pratt and Larned. Here Byers is pictured at center in the gray suit, posing with guests and A&N engine No. 2 on a gala occasion. But Byers' dream of a railroad empire was short lived. His line later struggled under the new name of the Wichita Northwestern and folded in 1940. Lee Berglund collection.

Machines and loads that could not have been imagined in 1867 continue to roll past the gravesites of six UPED trackworkers killed August 1 that year in a skirmish with Cheyenne Indians near what is now Victoria, Kansas. Located south of the right of way at Victoria, a history marker erected by the Union Pacific and weather-faded individual tombstones attest to the toll extracted to complete the railroad. **Jim Reisdorff.**

Bibliography

Arkansas Valley Railway, by Philip J. Petersen; printed by PSP Enterprises, La Junta, Colo.,1993.

Boss, Michael, personal interviews and correspondence, 1998.

Collections of Kansas State Historical Society, "Early Days on the Union Pacific," by John D. Cruise; Volume XI; Topeka, 1910.

Denver Westerners Monthly Roundup, "A Prairie Town of Train Robbers," by Stanley W. Zamonski; Volume XIX No. 6, June 1963.

Ghost Towns of Kansas, by Daniel Fitzgerald; University Press of Kansas, 1988.

Guide Map of the Great Texas Cattle Trail, published by the Kansas Pacific Railway, 1874; reproduced by the Kansas State Historical Society, 1973.

Historical Guide to North American Railroads, by George H. Drury; Kalmbach Books, 1991 (1985).

History of the Atchison, Topeka and Santa Fe, by Keith L. Bryant, Jr.; University of Nebraska Press, 1982.

History of Wallace County, Kansas, by the Wallace County History Book Committee; Curtis Media Corporation, 1991.

Journeys Through Western Rail History; Colorado Rail

Annual No. 22, "The Lost Locomotive of Kiowa Creek," by Loyd J. Glasier; Colorado Railroad Museum, 1997.

Kansas: A Cyclopedia of State History ..., edited by Frank W. Blackmar; Standard Publications, Chicago, 1912.

Kansas: A History, by Kenneth S. Davis; W.W. Norton and Company, 1984 (1976).

Kansas Depots, by H. Roger Grant; Kansas State Historical Society, 1990.

Kansas in the Sixties, by Samuel J. Crawford; A.C. McClurg and Company, 1911; reprinted by Kansas Heritage Press, 1994.

Kansas Historical Collections, 1926-1928, "When Railroading Outdid the Wild West Stories," by O. P. Byers, 1928.

Kansas Historical Quarterly, "Along the Line of the Kansas Pacific Railway in Western Kansas in 1870"; *Volume XIX, No. 2, May 1951.*

ibid. "Samuel Hallett and the Union Pacific Railway Company in Kansas," by Alan W. Farley; Volume XXV, No. 1, Spring 1959.

ibid. "When the Union and Kansas Pacific Built Through Kansas," by Joseph W. Snell and Robert W. Richmond; Volume XXXII, No. 2, Summer 1966.

A number of the photographs taken by Robert Beneke on his tour of the Kansas Pacific were later painstakingly copied as line illustrations to allow for reproduction in newspapers of the period. Such was done with this view of Russell, Kansas, circa 1874. From such humble conditions would come a rail line that continues to serve as a vital part of Union Pacific's modern freight operations.
Union Pacific Museum.

ibid. "When the Union and Kansas Pacific Built Through Kansas, Part 2," by Joseph W. Snell and Robert W. Richmond; Volume XXXII, No. 3, Autumn 1966.

Kansas Pacific Railroad, by Waldo Crippen; Arno Press, 1981.

Kansas West, by George L. Anderson; Golden West Books (Pacific Railroad Publications), 1963.

Lela Barnes Railroad Collection, Kansas State Historical Society microfilm record, MS 1312 and 1313; ca. 1971.

Military correspondence of Fort Hays: from Fort Hays State Historical Site, administerd by the Kansas State Historical Society.

More True Tales of Old-Time Kansas, by David Dary; University Press of Kansas, 1987.

Rocky Mountain News: March 31, 1870; August 16, 1870; December 8, 1870; January 27, 1876; and September 27, 1879.

The Sea Hunters, by Clive Cussler and Craig Dirgo; Pocket Star Books (Simon and Schuster), 1997.

Story of the Western Railroads, by Robert Edgar Riegel; University of Nebraska Press, 1964 (MacMillan Company, 1926).

Trails of the Smoky Hill: From Coronado to the Cowtowns, by Wayne C. Lee and Howard C. Raynesford; Caxton Printers, 1980.

True Tales of Old-Time Kansas, by David Dary; University Press of Kansas, 1984.

Treasure, "The Locomotive That Vanished"; Volume 20, No. 7, July 1989.

Union Pacific Country, by Robert G. Athearn; Rand McNally & Company, 1971.

Union Pacific Magazine, June 1931; July 1931.

Unsere Leute 100, by Norbert R. Dreiling; Volga-German Centennial Association, 1976.

Victoria - The Story of a Western Kansas Town, by Marjorie Gamet Raish; Topeka, Kans., 1947.

West of Wichita, by Craig Miner; University Press of Kansas, 1986.

Wild, Woolly & Wicked, by Harry Sinclair Drago; Clarkson N. Potter Incorporated, 1960.

In a dramatic contrast to a Kansas Pacific passenger train of old, the Union Pacific's eastbound "Denver Limited" paused at Sharon Springs during the 1940's. The unidentified UP trainman was reported to be on his last run, concluding a career along the former Kansas Pacific route that generations of railroaders have similarly followed before and since. The reason for including the new Chrysler automobile is unknown. However, it does suggest where the future of public passenger transportation was then headed. Union Pacific Museum.